Love Set Free

Love Set Free

Meditations on the Passion
According to John

Martin L. Smith, SSJE

COWLEY PUBLICATIONS
Cambridge ✦ Boston
Massachusetts

© 1998 Martin L. Smith, SSJE

Library of Congress Cataloging-in-Publication Data:
Smith, Martin Lee.

Love set free: meditations on the passion according to John/ Martin L. Smith.

    p.   cm.

Includes bibliographic references.

ISBN 1-56101-153-3 (alk. paper)

1. Bible. N.T. John XIX—Meditations. 2. Jesus Christ—Passion—Meditations. I. Title.

| BS2615.4.S64   1998 | 98-25268 |
| 232.96—dc21 | CIP |

Biblical quotations are taken from the *New Revised Standard Version* of the Bible, ©1989.

Cynthia Shattuck, editor; Vicki Black, copyeditor and designer. Cover art by Georges Rouault, *Crucifixion*, c. 1914.

This book is printed on recycled, acid-free paper and was produced in Canada.   *Second printing*

Cowley Publications   •   28 Temple Place
Boston, Massachusetts 02111
800-225-1534   •   http://www.cowley.org

To Alan Grainge, SSJE
with affection and gratitude.

Contents

Introduction

I was invited in 1997 to give a series of meditations on the passion of Christ at Trinity Church, Boston, during the Good Friday service that lasts from noon to three o'clock. Traditionally the addresses in this service offer reflections on each of the "seven last words" of Jesus from the cross, gathered from all four gospels. Instead of following this convention I chose to lead the worshipers in meditation through the passion narrative of a single gospel, the gospel of John. There was a reason for this other than the fact that the particular dedication of the religious community to which I belong, the Society of St. John the Evangelist, is a constant incentive to introduce others to the riches of the fourth gospel. I also wanted to be more faithful in meditative preaching to one of the most significant advances in biblical interpretation of this century.

In recent decades scholars have become sharply aware of the distinctive character of each of the gospels. In the past Christians have tended, usually unconsciously but sometimes deliberately, to underplay the differences in style and content among the gospels and to blend them together. In the early centuries writers produced harmonies of the gospels, composite works that wove stories and sayings from all four gospels into one narrative. The same instincts were at work in Christian art, storytelling, preaching, liturgy, drama, and theology, so that by now this blending of the four sources has become second nature to us. For example, even though strict examination shows that the stories of Jesus' birth in Luke and Matthew are really different traditions, rather than elements that simply slot together into a whole, Christmas devotion in all its expressions quite happily combines these alternative traditions. In the same way, when we think of the passion narrative, our minds instinctively weave together elements from all four of the gospels.

Now it has become startlingly clear that each gospel writer brought to the work a unique artistry. Each gospel has a set of distinctive religious standpoints and emphases, partly reflecting the different character of the community for which it was written and partly the theological artistry of the writer. (More accurately, we should speak of writers and editors in the plural—there is evidence, especially in the case of the fourth gospel, that the book has gone through several stages of composition.) Treating each gospel separately in our study of the Bible, learning to compare and contrast them, and differentiating among them allows us to appreciate much more vividly the urgent religious intention of each writer, and the distinctive situation and mission of the community to which each belonged. Harmonizing the gospels is second nature to us, but if we reverse that trend to heighten our sense of their uniqueness we begin to see that harmonizing can have the effect of blurring and diluting their impact. If someone were to take a computer image of a biblical scene by Rembrandt and another of the same scene by El Greco and "morph" them into a composite image, we would recoil from the grotesque result and condemn the project as perverse. That is because works of art communicate with us in very rich and subtle ways by the innumerable elements of style that are distinctive to the artist.

Far from being chiefly of interest to scholars, the great gains of the last few decades in identifying the distinctive characteristics of each gospel are a great gift to our religious experience, our spirituality. Meditation as a spiritual discipline is above all the art of focused receptivity. It is the discipline of suspending our tendency to control and censor, allowing ourselves to be vulnerable to the impact of images and symbols so that they can bring grace to bear on our inmost selves. In contemplating the images and scenes and words of scripture, we allow the same kind of process to occur as when we place ourselves before a great work of art, not to criticize or analyze it, but to be open to its transforming power.

If you are not familiar with the differences between the four gospel accounts of Christ's final days, you may find it helpful to compare them. It makes a fascinating Bible study for a group of people to do together. For example, it soon becomes apparent that Luke's account of the final events of Jesus' life bear the fingerprints of the evangelist's particular interests. Luke emphasizes Jesus' ministry as a healer, so we find that alone among the evangelists he mentions that Jesus healed the ear of the high priest's slave after one of the disciples had cut it off in the scuffle to prevent Jesus' arrest (22:50-51). Luke is especially interested in Jesus' relationship with women, so he alone describes how on the way to execution Jesus spoke with a group of grieving women (23:27-31). Mark grimly records that the two bandits crucified with Jesus taunted him, but Luke, wishing to depict Jesus as compassionate reconciler, shows him promising the fellow sufferer who asked to be remembered in Jesus' kingdom, "Truly I tell, you, today you will be with me in Paradise" (23:43). Unlike Mark, who has Jesus uttering a final agonizing cry of desolation, "My God, my God, why have you forsaken me?" (Mark 15:34), Luke prefers to show Jesus as the faithful Son who surrenders himself to God in death, saying, "Father, into your hands I commend my spirit" (23:46).

John's account of Jesus' last days also differs in many ways from the other gospels. Jesus' cleansing of the temple is not the climactic event that it is in the other gospels because John daringly chose to transfer it to the very beginning of Jesus' ministry. Nor does his account of the last supper make any mention of Jesus' actions and words over the bread and wine that were the origins of the eucharist. Instead, the evangelist makes the dramatic sign of self-giving love in Jesus' washing of the disciples' feet the focus of the event, and pictures the supper as the final opportunity for Jesus to instruct and initiate the disciples. It concludes with the serene and magnificent prayer in which Jesus offers to God a summary of his mission and prepares for his return to God's presence.

Throughout the gospel John portrays Jesus not as the victim of a plot, but rather as one who retains the initiative right to the last. "For this reason the Father loves me, because I lay down my life in order to take it up again. No one takes it from me, but I lay it down of my own accord. I have power to lay it down, and I have power to take it up again" (10:17-18). Jesus is able to discern when "the hour has come for the Son of Man to be glorified" (12:23). He is not immune to pain and horror in the face of his betrayal and rejection—"Now is my soul troubled. And what should I say—'Father, save me from this hour'?" (12:27)—but he remains aware of his union with God and this carries him through his arrest, interrogation, torture, and death. The awesome authority with which this awareness invests Jesus is conveyed dramatically in the thrilling simplicity with which he identifies himself to the soldiers who have come to arrest him: "I am" (18:5). As on all the other occasions where Jesus identifies himself in this way, John wants to remind us of God's disclosure of his identity to Moses in the burning bush, I AM WHO I AM. So John has the soldiers stepping back and falling to the ground at these words, as if instinctively recognizing that in Jesus they are dealing with more than a mere mortal.

The following six meditations are not meant to be read through at one sitting. Each one is best appreciated and used when it can be followed by a time of reflection and prayer. The first meditation is based on the beginning of chapter 19. In preparation you might find it helpful to read the whole of John's gospel up to that point, or at least from chapter 12, verse 20 on, when the movement towards the cross begins to gather momentum. Some of you will spread your use of these meditations over a long period, perhaps during the whole season of Lent, allowing several days for each one to sink in. Others may want to set aside periods of reflection during Holy Week. If you are unable to take part in worship on Good Friday, you may want to find some time alone that day and use all the meditations together as the vehicle for your prayer.

The meditations are not exercises in biblical interpretation. Rather, they are invitations to allow the images that John has gathered together in a unique way to resonate deeply in your imagination. Think of them as similar to the comments that an art critic would write for the catalog of a show of paintings, which are intended not to dictate the response of the viewers, but rather to help stimulate and clarify the feelings to which the paintings give rise. My hope is that these short meditations, with the scripture passages and poetry selections, will bring the images of Jesus' passion into sharper focus for you, and act as a stimulus to prayer.

At the very end of his gospel John himself says that no account of the mystery of Jesus can ever be complete: "There are also many other things that Jesus did; if every one of them were written down, I suppose that the world itself could not contain the books that would be written" (21:25). These meditations are offered in the belief that all of us who are prepared to be caught up in the story are the authors of these unwritten books, using the language of prayer.

one

Embodiment

"Here is the man!"

John 19:1-16a

Then Pilate took Jesus and had him flogged. And the
soldiers wove a crown of thorns and put it on his head,
and they dressed him in a purple robe. They kept
coming up to him, saying, "Hail, King of the Jews!"
and striking him on the face. Pilate went out again and
said to them, "Look, I am bringing him out to you to
let you know that I find no case against him." So Jesus
came out, wearing the crown of thorns and the purple
robe. Pilate said to them, "Here is the man!" When the
chief priests and the police saw him, they shouted,
"Crucify him! Crucify him!" Pilate said to them, "Take
him yourselves and crucify him; I find no case against
him." The Jews answered him, "We have a law, and
according to that law he ought to die because he has
claimed to be the Son of God."

Now when Pilate heard this, he was more afraid than
ever. He entered his headquarters again and asked
Jesus, "Where are you from?" But Jesus gave him no
answer. Pilate therefore said to him, "Do you refuse to
speak to me? Do you not know that I have power to

release you, and power to crucify you?" Jesus answered him, "You would have no power over me unless it had been given you from above; therefore the one who handed me over to you is guilty of a greater sin." From then on Pilate tried to release him, but the Jews cried out, "If you release this man, you are no friend of the emperor. Everyone who claims to be a king sets himself against the emperor."

When Pilate heard these words, he brought Jesus outside and sat on the judge's bench at the place called The Stone Pavement, or in Hebrew Gabbatha. Now it was the day of Preparation for the Passover; and it was about noon. He said to the Jews, "Here is your King!" They cried out, "Away with him! Away with him! Crucify him!" Pilate asked them, "Shall I crucify your King?" The chief priests answered, "We have no king but the emperor." Then he handed him over to them to be crucified.

Embodiment

The gospel of John is the only one that identifies an eyewitness source for the narrative of Jesus' passion. The narrator could have revealed the identity of his source at the beginning of the story, but he waits until a particular moment to reveal that it is the disciple whom Jesus loved, the man who dared to keep company with the mother of Jesus at the foot of the cross, who speaks to us. John tells us, "He who saw this has testified so that you also may believe. His testimony is true, and he knows that he tells the truth" (19:35). This moment of identification comes after Jesus' death on the cross, as soon as his body is pierced by the soldier's spear, letting forth a stream of blood and water.

This image of penetration from outside to the inmost place of Jesus' own heart is a mysterious sign of the character of the fourth gospel. This gospel penetrates the surface of the events of Jesus' life, death, and resurrection to reach into the hidden depths, the *insideness* of it all.

The story of Jesus' passion can be told as a drama, a passion play, whose impact comes from the way it seizes our imaginations and stirs up our feelings through the unfolding of vivid scene after vivid scene. Lurid details can draw us into the events as spellbound spectators. But John's gospel is not an invitation to undergo the pathos and catharsis of a dramatic spectacle like the famous passion play of Oberammagau, with its wrenching reenactment of the crucifixion. Instead, it is an invitation to surrender ourselves to a movement into the hidden depths of it all.

No one could make a movie from John's narrative. The story is not intended to sweep us along on the surface through a succession of gripping images. To produce a pictorial equivalent of this gospel we would have to invent a strange new artwork, perhaps a complex sequence of images of the kind produced by medical technologies such as X-ray, CAT scan, ultrasound, MRI. All these technologies penetrate the surface to produce different kinds of images that allow us to know the inner depths, the places hidden from sight. It is only through meditation that these images from the deep inner structure of Jesus' passion story reveal their meaning. We hold them up to the light to scan them with the eyes of our soul. It is then that we come to know that they are the images revealing our own depths, the truth of our own selves, our own origins, our own identities, our own destinies.

Such an image is given to us in the moment recorded by John when Pilate displays Jesus to the crowd, saying, "Here is the man!" Jesus stands there motionless in the costume of mockery. He is crowned with thorns and wears a cloak of regal purple. He has been flogged, and blood soaks through his clothes from the lacerations of the savage whip. In the stillness of this moment John wants to focus our attention through the irony of the announcement, "Here is the man." On the surface, Pilate's declaration seems to be a simple attempt to get the crowd's attention. He wants them to *see* Jesus, to see that he is too broken and absurd a man to be a king. Here is the man you all are accusing, Pilate says. How could he possibly be guilty as charged?

Ironically, Pilate is giving away a deeper truth. This is *the* human being. This is the real human person. His declaration unwittingly reminds us that Jesus used to call himself, enigmatically, the Son of Man. This Semitic idiom would be better translated "the Human One." The expression can be used simply as a way of referring to oneself as a human being—"this guy here"—but it had other overtones as well. Visionaries such as the writer of the book of Daniel used the title Son of Man for a heavenly figure who was the embodiment and representative of God's people. Jesus seems to have expected people to identify him as this representative figure who was so completely identified with humanity that his fate would change the destiny of us all: "For the Son of Man came not to be served but to serve, and to give his life a ransom for many" (Mark 10:45).

Because Jesus is the Son of Man, the Human One, our representative, he is a mirror in which we can see the reflection of our true identity. So we are able to look at the image of Jesus being brought out before the crowd and see in him what we have made of our own humanity. To be human is to have inherited a royal state in creation, a state of awareness that distinguishes us from other creatures: the sovereign condition of responsibility for one another and for our earth. So the psalmist wonders aloud why God so values the son of man, that is, the human race:

> What is man
>> that you should be mindful of him,
> the son of man
>> that you should seek him out?
> You have made him
>> but little lower than the angels;
> You adorn him
>> with glory and honor.
>>>> (*BCP*, Psalm 8:4-5)

The subject of our royal grandeur is a tragic one because we only know that sovereignty in a ruined state. Human beings have a thousand ways of using their power to degrade, humiliate, and destroy one another. This cycle of violence and negation is fueled by an inner source of self-destructiveness present in the human heart. It is our hatred of our own selves that we act out upon one another. It is our own dignity we ravage with cynicism. We flog our own beauty with negation, and crown ourselves and one another with rings of thorns that pierce our brows with pain and fill our eyes with blood. "Here is the human one!" Jesus personifies us as victim of humanity turned against itself. This figure is our own savaged humanity.

In the letter to the Hebrews, the writer summons us with these words to contemplate Jesus in his suffering: "Consider him who endured such hostility against himself from sinners" (12:3). Or at least that is the translation we commonly find. But in fact some of the most ancient manuscripts have this version: "Consider him who endured such hostility from sinners *against themselves.*" Exactly. The writer puts his finger right on the wound. The hostility unleashed on Jesus, the hostility that framed him and forced his cruel, degrading execution, unmasks our own hostility against ourselves, our own self-destruction. In Jesus we sense the very fullness and grandeur of the humanity we are helplessly bent on wounding and killing in ourselves.

But the irony of the proclamation "Here is the man!" goes even further. In John's gospel the reason for Jesus' condemnation is that he made himself equal to God. "He ought to die because he has claimed to be the Son of God," the Jews told Pilate (19:7). Jesus is the man who said that to see him is to see the Father, for he and the Father are one. Later in the gospel Thomas' response to the sight of the wounds in the risen body of Jesus will be, "My Lord and my God!" At the sight of Jesus it is equally true to say "Here is God" and "Here is the man." The inner meaning of "Here is the man" is "here is the one who is really human because he is one with God. To be human is to be divine!"

The words of the Russian philosopher Nicholas Berdyaev are a good commentary on this moment of revelation in the passion story. In *The Divine and the Human* Berdyaev wrote:

> True humanness is likeness to God, it is the divine in man....In order to be

completely like man, it is necessary to be like God. It is necessary to have the divine image in order to have the human image. Man as we know him is but to a small extent human; he is even inhuman. It is not man who is human but God. It is God who requires of man that he should be human; man on his part makes very little demand for it. In exactly the same way, it is God who demands that man should be free, and not man himself.

"Here is the man!" We look at Jesus wearing the crown of thorns and the purple robe, using all his strength simply to stand, and the eyes of the heart see in him our own savaged and victimized humanity. But gazing at him longer and more deeply, we also see in the dignity of his stillness and suffering the compassion and companionship of God. God is not a distant God looking down at this scene, or a remote God peering over the horizon. If we really see Jesus, we see God and we see the unbroken oneness of Father and Son. "I and the Father are one." Only by drawing near enough to us to be caught up in the cycle of human self-destructive violence does God get near enough to end the cycle with healing, reconciliation, and reunion. In Jesus, bleeding under the crown of thorns and mockingly robed in purple, we see our own humanity wounded and weakened by our self-hatred. And if we are prepared to look into the hidden depths, we see in him the possibility of the restoration of our own humanity through the gift of divinity, the gift of God's union with us and presence to us here and now in the real world.

Love Set Free

Glory to you, O my Lord,
   who created us even though there was no cause
      for you to do so at any time;
glory to you, O my Lord,
   who called us your living image and likeness;
glory to you, my Lord,
   who nurtured us in freedom as rational beings;
glory to you, O just Father,
   whose love was pleased to fashion us;
glory to you, O holy Son,
   who put on our flesh and saved us;
glory to you, O living Spirit,
   who enriched us with your gifts;
glory to you, O hidden nature,
   who revealed yourself in our humanity.

—Syrian Orthodox Prayer

two

Vulnerability

"There they crucified him with two others."

John 19:16b-25a

So they took Jesus; and carrying the cross by himself, he went out to what is called The Place of the Skull, which in Hebrew is called Golgotha. There they crucified him, and with him two others, one on either side, with Jesus between them. Pilate also had an inscription written and put on the cross. It read, "Jesus of Nazareth, the King of the Jews." Many of the Jews read this inscription, because the place where Jesus was crucified was near the city; and it was written in Hebrew, in Latin, and in Greek....

When the soldiers had crucified Jesus, they took his clothes and divided them into four parts, one for each soldier. They also took his tunic; now the tunic was seamless, woven in one piece from the top. So they said to one another, "Let us not tear it, but cast lots for it to see who will get it." This was to fulfill what the scripture says, "They divided my clothes among themselves, and for my clothing they cast lots." And that is what the soldiers did.

The style of John's account of Jesus' crucifixion is calm and sober. This coolness is not meant to numb the pain. Rather, it invites us to recognize that any attempt at a realistic description of the crucifixion would fall so far short as to be absurd. Even if we could be transported back in time in order to witness it all, it is unlikely we would see very much. Most of the time we would be doubled over, retching our stomachs out from the stench of the victims' excrement. We would try to avert our eyes from the hideous sight of three men being tortured to death, heaving their bodies up on their nailed hands and feet to draw breath, an effort that each time costs them lightning bolts of agony. If we were strong enough not to faint, we would probably drift into a state of shock, reduced to gazing numbly at the faces of those around us—ordinary people with the ordinary cruelty of those who find the sadistic rituals of capital punishment irresistibly fascinating.

John does not pretend to conjure up the scene in its horror, but simply draws the bare outline with a few strokes. Jesus carries the crossbar himself to Golgotha, The Place of the Skull. He is crucified between two others. The cross has a notice-board in three languages that ironically proclaim his sovereignty. The executioners get his clothing as a perk. We are not meant to fill out this bare outline with detail, but rather to let the Spirit recall Jesus' words from earlier in the gospel that interpret the event and penetrate its inner meaning.

Much earlier in his ministry Jesus had pointed ahead to the passion, using the allusive language of "being lifted up." To Nicodemus, who came to him by night seeking a teacher, Jesus had said, "And just as Moses lifted up the serpent in the wilderness, so must the Son of Man be lifted up, that whoever believes in him may have eternal life" (3:14-15). In the temple at the Festival of Booths he had taught the crowd, "When you have lifted up the Son of Man, then you will realize that I am" (8:28). Finally, in recent days, he had addressed those who had come up for the Feast of the Passover: "And I, when I am lifted up from the earth, will draw all people to myself." And John adds, "He said this to indicate the kind of death he was to die" (12:32-33).

Crucifixion lifts its victim up to display him naked and immobilized. In John's gospel, Jesus' earlier words about being lifted up are premonitions of the fate awaiting him. But the language of being lifted up has other levels of meaning, too. The lifting up of Jesus on the cross is part of a single movement, part of his lifting up in his resurrection from the dead and his exaltation and ascension to union with God. The resurrection is in the cross, the ascension is in the cross, and the cross is in the resurrection and the ascension. It is one single raising up of the Son of Man. So the crucifixion on Golgotha is intensely ironic. It appears on the surface that Jesus is the victim who is being put down. But inadvertently the executioners are actually lifting Jesus up into his victory and glory. And being lifted up on the cross releases him. It is the trigger of resurrection, the raising of the dead, his and our reunion with God.

Further ironies await us. The crucifixion is a nauseating, repulsive event. But whereas on the surface the crucifixion repels, in inner reality it is the focal point to which we find ourselves irresistibly drawn by the attractiveness of God. In the third chapter of his gospel John shows Jesus reminding Nicodemus of one of the stories from the book of Numbers about the wilderness wandering of Israel. When venomous snakes attack the people, God instructs Moses to create a remarkable remedy. He fashions a bronze serpent and displays it to those who are dying from the snake bites. According to the legend, those who gazed on the bronze serpent were healed and saved from certain death. "And just as Moses lifted up the serpent in the wilderness, so must the Son of Man be lifted up, that whoever believes in him may have eternal life" (3:14-15). John is mysteriously suggesting that, like those injured men and women, we are drawn to gaze at Jesus on the cross through the intuition that our fatal wound will be healed by the sight of him. To the outward eye, the sight of Jesus lifted up is sickening and deathly. To the inward eye, it is radiant with healing power.

"And I, when I am lifted up from the earth, will draw all people to myself" (12:32). This saying of Jesus is based on the most fundamental of all myths, one that points to a place where humanity can mount up and have access to the divine realm of glory and eternity—a mountain, a ladder, a tree—the place of spiritual ascent. The enemies of light and life may lift Jesus up on the tree of crucifixion, but by so doing they unintentionally establish that axis of connection between earth and heaven. Lifting Jesus up creates a vortex of spiritual attraction that is universal in scope and eternal in duration. Golgotha becomes the place of convergence towards which all creation is drawn, the vortex that pulls all things upwards towards unity with God.

John is communicating through these images his deep conviction that God has no coercive power. God cannot overpower us, nor force us in any direction. In the vulnerability of the cross God reveals that the only power that can change us is one that attracts us freely, with the offer of healing. The stock-in-trade images of conventional belief, which picture God as an emperor in the sky, the wrathful enforcer of law, the deity who sanctions the rule of the strong, are shown up in the light of the cross as projections and idols. God's only power lies in the attractiveness of life and light to those who yearn for them. The only role God can play in relation to our brokenness is that of healer. All God can do is radiate this attraction through and from the one who in this world remained steadfastly in that light even when he was being destroyed.

"When you have lifted up the Son of Man, then you will realize that I am" (8:28). Throughout John's gospel Jesus proclaims I AM. *"I am* the light of the world." *"I am* the way, the truth, and the life." "Before Abraham was, *I am."* These are all echoes of God's revelation of the divine name to Moses in the burning bush, I AM WHO I AM. With these sayings John is constantly inviting us into the mystery of Jesus' intimacy with God, the unity that enables him to embody and reveal the universal mystery of the divine presence in the here and the now. Here, contemplating Jesus lifted up on the cross, John invites us to realize that now, more than ever, he is the incarnation, the embodiment of divine presence. The I AM, the utter mystery of love, creativity, and light we stammeringly call God, is simply here, fully and without qualification. The I AM is here in Jesus, Jesus in his utter vulnerability, in his mortality, in his nakedness to us on the cross. God is wholly and absolutely present, not as a ruler, punisher, or judge, but as the divine presence that remains in unbroken unity with Jesus in his faithfulness.

But this interior secret of the passion of Christ, this deep structure, cannot be made obvious. John cannot pretend that this mystery is plain for all to see. It is only revealed to those who will meditate upon it. And so he offers for our meditation a mysterious sign from among the mundane events of Jesus' execution. The soldiers rummage through the clothes they have torn from the victims' bodies. They come across his tunic, which John describes as "seamless, woven in one piece from the top" (19:23). One of the soldiers holds it up for all to admire. It is too good to tear up, and they decide to cast lots for it. With breathtaking restraint the evangelist simply places this image of the seamless robe before our imaginations to see whether it will touch off a response in our hearts. What the soldiers take from Jesus is a sign of seamless unity, something whole, all of a piece, woven from the top to the bottom.

Deep within us the intuition stirs that this is a symbol of Jesus' own seamless intimacy with God, which remains untorn even in the midst of torture and death. It is a unity that is woven by God in one piece from top to bottom, a unity that is God's gift and self-expression. It is the mystery that we desire for ourselves. The wound we long to have healed is the tear in the fabric of our hearts that estranges us from the ground and source of our being, from the divine heart. It is the vision of Jesus' own intimacy and union that draws us to stay at the cross so that he might clothe us with the seamless robe of the humanity that has become truly human at last because it has been reunited with God.

Love Set Free

The great Creator of the worlds,
    the sovereign God of heaven,
his holy and immortal truth
    to all on earth hath given.

He sent no angel of his host
    to bear this mighty word,
but him through whom the worlds were made,
    the everlasting Lord.

He sent him not in wrath and power,
    but grace and peace to bring;
in kindness, as a king might send
    his son, himself a king.

He sent him down as sending God;
    in flesh to us he came;
as one with us he dwelt with us,
    and bore a human name.

He came as Savior to his own,
    the way of love he trod;

Vulnerability

he came to win us by good will,
    for force is not of God.

Not to oppress, but summon all
    their truest life to find,
in love God sent his Son to save,
    not to condemn mankind.

—Epistle to Diognetus

three

Intimacy

"When Jesus saw his mother
and the disciple whom he loved...."

John 19:25b-27

Meanwhile, standing near the cross of Jesus were his mother, and his mother's sister, Mary the wife of Clopas, and Mary Magdalene. When Jesus saw his mother and the disciple whom he loved standing beside her, he said to his mother, "Woman, here is your son." Then he said to the disciple, "Here is your mother." And from that hour the disciple took her into his own home.

Crucifixion was considered the cruelest form of capital punishment. The execution of Jesus was not intended merely to destroy him as an individual. Its purpose was to smash a movement, to dissolve a community gathering around him, to scatter his adherents and followers, to alienate sympathizers. The crucifixion was intended to wreak a havoc of estrangement, disillusionment, and disintegration among those whom Jesus had been attracting to himself. The hideous penalty of crucifixion was reserved for slaves, rebels, blasphemers—those considered the scum of society. Because the Jewish law pronounced a special curse upon those hung upon a tree, it also defiled its victim, who became a religious abomination from whom all faithful Jews should recoil.

For John, the irony is that the cross itself is the very place where the community of love is created. In the midst of his suffering, Jesus begins to weave this community from the small band of people who had the courage to keep company with him as he hung upon the cross, starting with his mother and the disciple whom he loved. From the cross where Jesus is drawing all to himself he begins to weave the community of those who will live from intimacy with himself, intimacy with God through him.

John never refers to Mary by name. She is always "his mother." So the gospel draws our attention to the mystery of her giving life and birth to Jesus. Only mothers can know what it means to conceive a life within oneself, to have a new human being come from one's own body. Only a mother can experience the passionate oneness of holding and feeding this creature who has come from within her. And only a mother can experience the mingling of pain and joy as the child achieves individuality and becomes a distinct self.

All four gospels invite us to enter into the mystery of the intimacy of Jesus with his mother, an intimacy that began in the womb with union and then had to pass through separation to become communion. So Luke shows us Mary experiencing the shock of Jesus' provocative gesture of independence when, as a boy, he stayed behind in the temple after a pilgrimage instead of returning with the family group (Luke 2:41-52). Matthew and Mark show us Mary and the family attempting to intervene in Jesus' ministry and hearing Jesus' piercing words that made their blood relationship secondary: "'Who are my mother and my brothers?' And looking at those who sat around him, he said, 'Here are my mother and my brothers! Whoever does the will of God is my brother and sister and mother'" (Mark 3:33-35; Matthew 12:46-50). And John depicts Jesus and Mary at Cana exchanging words that reveal Jesus still has to assert his own authority: "Woman, what concern is that to you and to me? My hour has not yet come" (John 2:4). The bond of love uniting mother and son at the cross was not an easy harmony that had never been disturbed or shaken. When Mary brought Jesus to the temple as an infant, Simeon had predicted that a sword would pierce her soul, and so it did when Jesus went his own way.

Standing at the foot of the cross with Mary is the disciple whom Jesus loved. Because he is never actually named, some scholars have supposed that John wrote him into the story to represent the ideal of true discipleship. We are clearer now that the beloved disciple was a real person. The last chapter of John's gospel may actually be a kind of appendix or epilogue added to the earlier version, with the purpose of helping the faithful come to terms with the death of this disciple whom Jesus loved. After describing Jesus' third appearance to the disciples and his conversation with Peter, John speaks of himself as "the one who had reclined next to Jesus at the supper." He notes that "the rumor spread in the community that this disciple would not die. Yet Jesus did not say to him that he would not die, but, 'If it is my will that he remain until I come, what is that to you?'" (21:23).

It seems likely that this disciple was a young man, probably not one of the twelve, with whom Jesus developed a profound friendship. It was he whom Jesus wanted to have closest to him at the last supper. Reclining next to him, he could lean affectionately on Jesus' chest. The image of this physical closeness sets up a mysterious resonance with an image the evangelist has used before for the eternal relationship of the Son with God the Father: "No one has ever seen God. It is God the only Son, who is close to the Father's heart, who has made him known" (1:18). Strictly speaking, the word translated here as "heart" means "breast." So the evangelist is suggesting that the friendship between Jesus and the disciple he especially loved was of such depth that it had become an expression of the divine union of Father and Son.

"When Jesus saw his mother and the disciple whom he loved standing beside her, he said to his mother, 'Woman, here is your son.' Then he said to the disciple, 'Here is your mother.' And from that hour the disciple took her into his own home." Out of his agony on the cross, Jesus gives them to one another to care for each other. But the evangelist does not intend us to suppose that our meditation is complete once we have appreciated the tenderness of Jesus' care for his loved ones. No, through his lifting up on the cross

Jesus is drawing all to himself, so this new household that he creates is meant to be seen as the symbolic nucleus of the church, the all-embracing family. By tracing the origin of the church to this relationship between Jesus' mother and his beloved friend, the evangelist is asking us to remember two things about the church's true identity.

First, the community that Jesus' lifting up brings into existence is not an institution. It is not an organization. John does not even use the word "church." It is a communion grounded in the common experience of intimacy with Christ. It is the household of those who abide in him. As Christ is heard to pray the night before his death, "As you, Father, are in me and I am in you, so may they be also in us.... I in them and you in me, that they may become completely one" (17:21, 23).

Second, John is telling us that the new community is grounded in a commitment to reciprocal care and mutual love. Our meditation is meant to lead us back to the scene of the foot-washing the night before, when Jesus demonstrated the self-spending mutual service, the utter disregard for all human rank and status, that was to be the sign of the new community. By showing us how Jesus summons this community into existence from the cross, the evangelist invites us to realize again that this mutual service is nothing pleasant or easy. The new community is not an inward-looking mutual admiration society, but a force-field of costly self-giving. It is where friends lay down their lives for one another. It is a field where seeds have to die if they are to bear much fruit.

Through this simple pledging of Mary to the beloved disciple and of him to Mary at the foot of the cross, the evangelist takes the new commandment to love one another and places it directly in the vortex of death and self-offering. By doing so John squeezes every remaining drop of sentimentality out of our understanding of love. Love, love—the word is always ringing in our ears, but when is it not mixed up with something else? Love and the desire to possess, love and the need to control, love and the need to be needed, love and the lust to absorb, love and condescension, love and narcissism. In the Christian mystery love itself must be crucified, must die to be reborn as the grace of communion, as love set free. In a mysterious sign the evangelist points to the new home of the beloved disciple as the place where this has happened, the household from which the church's authentic identity has its origin.

Love Set Free

Where charity and love are, there is God.
The Love of Christ has gathered us as one.
Let us rejoice and be glad in him.
Let us fear and love the living God
And in purity of heart let us love one another.

Where charity and love are, there is God.
When therefore we are gathered together
Let us not be divided in spirit.
Let bitter strife and discord cease between us;
Let Christ our God be present in our midst.

Where charity and love are, there is God.
With all the blessed may we see for ever
Thy face in glory, Jesus Christ our God.
Joy that is infinite and undefiled
For all the ages of eternity.

—Ubi caritas, Latin hymn

four

Desire

"I am thirsty."

John 19:28-30

After this, when Jesus knew that all was now finished, he said (in order to fulfill the scripture), "I am thirsty." A jar full of sour wine was standing there. So they put a sponge full of the wine on a branch of hyssop and held it to his mouth. When Jesus had received the wine, he said, "It is finished." Then he bowed his head and gave up his spirit.

Powerless and immobilized, the victims of crucifixion were dependent on the charity of those standing around them for any alleviation of the burning thirst that tortured them during the slow hours of their ordeal. Medicinal wines that slightly numbed the pain might be available, or just the sour wine that soldiers would bring along for the hot hours of waiting. To those around the cross, Jesus' thirst has nothing unusual about it. No doubt all three victims were croaking for drink and Jesus is lucky enough for someone to use a bunch of twigs to push a sponge full of sour wine up to his mouth. Of course he was thirsty.

But the thirst the evangelist want us to understand has no "of course" about it. Jesus deliberately keeps from revealing his thirst until he is aware that he is on the brink of death. "When Jesus knew that all was now finished, he said (in order to fulfill the scripture), 'I am thirsty.'" It is not that Jesus knew everything had been done, so now he could gain some final relief. No, Jesus' thirst is itself the final expression of his revelation, and the moment when his thirst is quenched brings everything to its climax.

Jesus is thirsty. The climax of his whole life is that his thirst is quenched. After that climax his mission is fulfilled and he lets go of life. "When Jesus had received the wine, he said, 'It is finished.' Then he bowed his head and gave up his spirit."

"I am thirsty." John does not tell us what this thirst means because to do so would be to short-circuit our own response. If we cannot discover this thirst within ourselves, if this thirst does not touch the intuition of our hearts, it rests on the surface of the story—just a matter of Jesus' dry mouth in the hour of his death.

What could our hearts tell us about this thirst? "Here is the man." Jesus is humanity in its thirst for union with the mystery of our Origin, the all-encompassing Life we name so inadequately God. "O God, you are my God; eagerly I seek you; my soul thirsts for you, my flesh faints for you, as in a barren and dry land where there is no water" (Psalm 63:1). Most of us succeed in explaining that thirst away and our culture supplies all sorts of rationalizations. This thirst is really nothing more, we say, than displaced sexual longing, wishful thinking, regression, evasive fantasy. We believe we can find solutions for our thirst in the satisfactions of our version of the "good life." Or we can turn to the harsher and simpler remedies of our drug of choice to numb the thirst.

Jesus chose to live without any blurring or drugging of the thirst for God, and without the pretense that other people or the good life can assuage it. He has lived openly, consciously, and immediately the human reality of thirsting for God. He opened up a space within himself and his life large enough for the human desire for God to open in all its unrestricted fullness. He lived to that point where desire for God has finally come into its own as the meaning of his humanity. As the Son of Man is lifted up so that we can see who we are, Jesus is simply thirsty for God without qualification. Absolutely thirsty. Jesus is all desire without restraint. Jesus' desire is our desire free of the constraints with which we rein it in.

But Jesus is also the Son of Man lifted up so that we can know who God is. It is precisely as a human being who lived freely, out of sheer desire for God, that Jesus is the embodiment of God, the Word made flesh. Therefore the thirst of Jesus, solemnly proclaimed from the cross as the climax of God's self-expression, is the disclosure of a thirsty God. Jesus is the embodiment of humanity thirsting for God. And precisely as that, Jesus is the incarnation of God, thirsting for us and for creation.

There is nothing necessarily radical about proclaiming the love of God. Hallmark cards tell us that God loves us. Who else is the American God but a kindly uncle from whom we can expect an indulgent smile (though he has darker moods)? The divine love revealed in Jesus' cry of thirst is not benevolence but desire—not desire that is mere wishing, but desire that is a burning thirst. "God so loved the world that he gave his only Son, so that everyone who believes in him may not perish but have eternal life" (John 3:16). This love is desire for us, a desire so intense that the desperate thirst of the crucified in agony is the only reality that will serve as a lens to focus that yearning for our heart's understanding.

Jesus proclaimed that in being lifted up he would draw all to himself. In his cry "I am thirsty," the energy that exerts itself upon us, the current that pulls us towards him in spite of our doubt and resistance, the undertow that carries us off our feet when we want to halt a distance away, is revealed as divine eros, God's thirst to bring us into union with himself.

Jesus laps at the soaking sponge, which is cradled in a bunch of hyssop. The stalks of this bitter herb were used for sprinkling blood and water in the solemn sacrificial rituals of purification and atonement. The evangelist gives us the name of the herb in passing in the hope that the symbol will expand in our souls through meditation. At this moment, when the thirst of Jesus is quenched at the very point of death, atonement, at-one-ment, has occurred because the human desire for God and God's desire for humanity is at one. These thirsts have converged into a single reality of being as one. Jesus and the Father are one. In this unity God's thirst for humanity is slaked, and so is our thirst for God.

At this moment nothing more remains to be done. All has been fulfilled. "When Jesus had received the wine, he said, 'It is finished.' Then he bowed his head and gave up his spirit." The evangelist chooses the words to express the moment of Jesus' death with great care: *paredoken to pneuma.* These words can mean "gave up breath." But breath means spirit, so here the translation could just as well be "handed over the Spirit." Standing beneath him, close enough for the whispered conversation about their new relationship, are his mother and the disciple whom Jesus loved. The Holy Spirit that is the living bond of intimacy between Jesus and the Father, the shared breathing of their union, Jesus now hands on to them. His death means that this spirit of at-one-ness is now released as a gift. No longer is it contained within the bounds of his own person. He releases it. Others begin to catch it.

Love Set Free

Glorious Lord Christ: you who are the first and the last, the living and the dead and the risen again; you who gather into your exuberant unity every mode of existence; it is you to whom my being cries out with a desire as vast as the universe, "In truth you are my Lord and my God."

—Teilhard de Chardin

five

Union

"One of the soldiers pierced his side."

John 19:31-37

Since it was the day of Preparation, the Jews did not want the bodies left on the cross during the sabbath, especially because that sabbath was a day of great solemnity. So they asked Pilate to have the legs of the crucified men broken and the bodies removed. Then the soldiers came and broke the legs of the first and of the other who had been crucified with him. But when they came to Jesus and saw that he was already dead, they did not break his legs. Instead, one of the soldiers pierced his side with a spear, and at once blood and water came out. (He who saw this has testified so that you also may believe. His testimony is true, and he knows that he tells the truth.) These things occurred so that the scripture might be fulfilled, "None of his bones shall be broken." And again another passage of scripture says, "They will look on the one whom they have pierced."

In John's narrative of the passion, no dramatic break occurs with the event of Jesus' death. The other gospels mark the climactic moment with pronouncements from the centurion about Jesus' innocence, or with dramatic effects like an earthquake and the rending of the temple veil from top to bottom. But John's narrative omits everything that might disrupt our contemplative expectancy. In dying, Jesus has handed over his spirit. Now we are to watch what happens next. There is more to come. The evangelist wants to focus our attention on a further event in the passion that is missing from the other three gospels.

This Friday is drawing rapidly towards dusk and the Jews who are anxious not to violate the Torah want to make sure that there will be time to dispose of the corpses before the onset of the sabbath. Under orders from Pilate, the soldiers administer the *coup de grace* to the two men being crucified with Jesus. With their legs broken they can no longer heave themselves up to breathe. Death follows swiftly. But Jesus is already dead.

One of the soldiers makes sure that Jesus is really dead by a quick spear thrust into his thorax. Body fluids that have accumulated there, blood and water, spurt out.

The evangelist then highlights the event as supremely significant: he reminds us that the disciple whom Jesus loved saw this and bore witness to it so that we might believe. It is, literally, a moment of truth: "His testimony is true, and he knows that he tells the truth." The spear-thrust appears on the surface of the story merely as a grotesque mutilation, a final indignity. But what is happening that we should pause here? What does this piercing of Jesus' body mean? What do the blood and water signify, that John should insist that the secret of belief is to be found here?

The evangelist has left the clue back in the seventh chapter of the gospel, where Jesus goes up to the temple for the Feast of Booths.

> On the last day of the festival, the great day, while Jesus was standing there, he cried out, "Let anyone who is thirsty

come to me, and let the one who believes in me drink. As the scripture has said, 'Out of his belly shall flow rivers of living water.'" Now he said this about the Spirit, which believers in him were to receive; for as yet there was no Spirit, because Jesus was not yet glorified. (John 7:37-39)

Earlier still in John's gospel, Jesus had promised the Samaritan woman at the well, "The water that I will give will become in them a spring of water gushing up to eternal life" (4:14). Now in the temple Jesus declares that this inner spring will flow from the interior, the belly. But the wording is ambiguous. Is this Jesus' belly or the believer's? Of course the ambiguity is deliberate, pointing forward to this moment. The lance thrust that causes water to flow from Jesus' belly is a symbolic key to the inner secret of Jesus' life of union with the Father.

The Spirit dwelt in him as a living, vital source, bearing him up into the fullness of intimacy with God. The physical fluid spurting out of the wound is a sign of the outflow of the Spirit within Jesus that is now pouring forth. The beloved disciple now realizes that Jesus' inner life has been opened up, made accessible to us. By flowing out of Jesus, it has come into us. Now the mystery of the indwelling Spirit is going to become our mystery. We are going to experience the same inner availability of the Spirit. "'Out of their bellies shall flow rivers of living water.' Now he said this about the Spirit, which believers in him were to receive."

After this speech in the temple earlier in the gospel, the evangelist tells us that as yet there was no Spirit because its release could occur only with the glorification of Jesus. But now on the cross Jesus has been lifted into glory and handed over his spirit. From now on Jesus' experience of the indwelling Spirit can become ours. In the upper room the risen Christ will breathe his spirit into his friends, but even now, the evangelist is telling us, the glorification has taken place and the water of the Spirit has gushed out, as water gushed out when Moses struck the rock in the wilderness with his staff.

So here in the midst of the passion, if we are willing to pause in contemplation at this moment when the spear cuts into Jesus' side, the beloved disciple will take us into the heart of the mystery. It is the mystery of baptism, our rebirthing by water and spirit. In baptism the inner personhood of Christ becomes ours. Abiding in us, he becomes the heart of our hearts, the self of our selves. His experience of indwelling Spirit becomes our experience, his union with the Father becomes our union.

It is not water only that flows out from the wound but blood, the witnessing disciple tells us, Jesus' life-blood. Earlier in the sixth chapter of John's gospel, Jesus is shown teaching in the synagogue at Capernaum. There Jesus claims that the manna in the wilderness was not the real bread from heaven, but that he himself is the life-giving, divine bread. He stuns his listeners by offering his body as food and his blood as drink:

> Very truly, I tell you, unless you eat the flesh of the Son of Man and drink his blood, you have no life in you. Those who

eat my flesh and drink my blood have
eternal life, and I will raise them up on the
last day; for my flesh is true food and my
blood is true drink. Those who eat my
flesh and drink my blood abide in me, and
I in them. Just as the living Father sent
me, and I live because of the Father, so
whoever eats me will live because of me.
(6:53-57)

This life-blood of Jesus is to be taken into us,
sacramentally drunk and absorbed so that we live
from communion with him.

Now, at the solemn climax of the passion
narrative, the evangelist touches us with another
mysterious allusion to the eucharist. Those who are
willing to follow him in meditation are led into an
awesome realization of the meaning of the
eucharistic cup. This eucharist is no mere
fellowship meal or vague memorial. It is a matter of
life and death. It is nothing less than taking into
ourselves the very person and life of Jesus glorified,
so that his union with God becomes ours through
his abiding in us.

To follow the passion according to John is to allow ourselves a mystical experience; there is no other word for it. Everything in the gospel returns over and over again to this one mystery of faith. Believing is not a matter of acknowledging the existence of God, or even of "having a relationship" with God, however devout. Nor is it an external affair of obeying, following, serving, or imitating Jesus. Belief is admission of Christ into ourselves, as it is our admission into his self. And so the passion narrative culminates in this mysterious, even savage, sign of Jesus' being opened up, thrust into. Faith is the mystery of our being entered. Faith is the act of recognition that we cannot any longer defend ourselves against the interiority of God in us. We cannot any longer pretend that God is located out there or up there or back there. In believing we realize that our bellies, our guts, have been opened up, and there God is at home in us, in Jesus, through the Spirit.

Union

Love in the fountain and love in the stream are both the same. And therefore are they both equal in time and glory. For love communicateth itself, and therefore love in the fountain is the very love communicated to its object.

Love in the fountain is love in the stream, and love in the stream is equally glorious with love in the fountain. Though it streameth to its object, it abideth in the lover, and is the love of the lover.

—Thomas Traherne, "Thanksgivings"

six

Silence

"The tomb was nearby, they laid Jesus there."

John 19:38-42

After these things, Joseph of Arimathea, who was a disciple of Jesus, though a secret one because of his fear of the Jews, asked Pilate to let him take away the body of Jesus. Pilate gave him permission; so he came and removed his body. Nicodemus, who had at first come to Jesus by night, also came, bringing a mixture of myrrh and aloes, weighing about a hundred pounds. They took the body of Jesus and wrapped it with the spices in linen cloths, according to the burial custom of the Jews. Now there was a garden in the place where he was crucified, and in the garden there was a new tomb in which no one had ever been laid. And so, because it was the Jewish day of Preparation, and the tomb was nearby, they laid Jesus there.

Psalm 115 calls the dead "those who go down into silence." So Good Friday draws to its close in silence with Jesus' burial in the nearby tomb. Jesus has passed in death beyond the reach of language or imagination. Nothing that can be said or imagined has the strength to withstand the silence of the unknown into which he has passed. The Word through whom all things came into being was made flesh and lived among us; he is Jesus. Now Jesus is dead. What can we say? Poetry can lead us to the place of wonder, but it patrols the shoreline of what can be said, only making us more aware of the ocean of the unsayable. The poetry inspired by the passion always takes us to the edge of silence, as in these words translated from one of the great hymns of the Welsh mystic Ann Griffiths:

> He is the satisfaction between the thieves,
> he suffered the pains of death, it was he
> who gave to the arms of his executioners
> the power to nail him there to the cross;
> when he pays the debt of brands plucked
> out of the burning, and honours his

Father's law, Righteousness shines with
fiery blaze as it pardons within the terms
of the free reconciliation.

O my soul, behold the place where lay the
chief of kings, the author of peace, all
creation moving in him, and he lying
dead in the tomb; song and life of the lost,
greatest wonder of the angels of heaven,
the choir of them see God in flesh and
worship him together, crying out "Unto
him."

"The author of all peace, all creation moving in
him, and he lying dead in the tomb."

At the beginning of John's gospel, Jesus
appears out of silence. John the Baptist identifies
him as "the Lamb of God who takes away the sin
of the world" (1:29). And now, at the end of the
gospel, Jesus is laid in the tomb. But what has the
evangelist said about this taking away of the sin of
the world? Where is his explanation of how Jesus'
death does that? Where is the theory for such a
claim? Surely Good Friday cannot end without

some account of the *how* of atonement. But atonement is not explained; Jesus is laid in the tomb and the rest is silence.

The evangelist has not forgotten the claim he makes at the beginning of his gospel: "Here is the Lamb of God who takes away the sin of the world!" But John offers no theory of atonement. Instead, he bears witness to the experience of it. None of us can understand how the self-offering of Christ on the cross can take away the sin of the world unless we have experienced our own sin being taken away. And this experience is the experience of oneness with Christ as a gift. Sin is all that is done in the illusory state of estrangement from God. With the gift of at-one-ment, sin is taken away. No one who receives this gift can believe in any limit to the power of God to overcome alienation. No one who is forgiven and accepted in the experience of Christ abiding in us and we abiding in Christ can then say, "Ah, yes, in my case, the Lamb of God has taken away sin, but as for others, maybe that will be impossible."

To believe is to have crossed over into the limitless and eternal life of divine compassion. To believe is to be united to the All-encompassing and Unbounded. There can be no taking away of sin that is not able to take away *all* sin. It is all or nothing. Because it has happened to us, then we know it is available for all. In the experience of atonement we experience our own selves as a microcosm of the whole. God leaves no part of ourselves untouched by forgiveness, gently passing through the inmost doors that are shut tight from fear. So we know at the deepest level of faith that there is no part of creation powerful enough to shut out divine compassion. The Son of Man will draw all to himself.

The gospel leaves us today in the silence of the tomb with the falling of night. This is a silence that nothing can break except the resurrection. Only Christ can break this silence with his words of greeting: "Mary!" "Peace be with you!" We must wait in silence for the first day of the week. But for John the glorification is already underway. Already transformation is at work. Even the meaning of night has changed. Night itself becomes a sign of hope and grace. What used to be the ceaseless reminder of extinction has now become the sign of God's all-encompassing compassion. The silence of the night is the divine quietness that stills the deafening racket of accusation and blame. The darkness of the night has become a sign of God's gift to us of ultimate rest and relief from the exhausting work of self-destructiveness and self-justification.

In his poem "The Mystery of the Holy Innocents," Charles Péguy lets God speak to us of the promise implicit in the darkness and silence that brings Good Friday to an end. The night of God's mourning, the Good Friday night of God's desolation at the death of his Son, is the night that frees him to promise us a close to our seemingly endless day of ingratitude and crime.

Silence

O night, must it be, then must it be that my Paradise
Will be nothing but a great clear night
    which will fall on the sins of the world. . . .
And all that I shall be able to offer
As my gift and as my offertory
To so many martyrs and so many executioners,
To so many souls and to so many bodies,
To so many pure and to so many impure,
To so many sinners and to so many saints
To so many faithful and to so many penitents,
And for so much pain and for so much mourning and
    for so many tears and for so many wounds,
And to so many hearts who have throbbed so much
    with love, with hate,
And to so many hearts who have bled so much
    with love, with hate,
Shall it be said that it must be
That I must offer them
And they will ask nothing but that,
    That they will want nothing but that,
    That they will have no desire for anything but that,
On those stains and on so much bitterness,

Love Set Free

And on that immense sea of ingratitude
The slow fall of an eternal night?

—The Mystery of the Innocents and Other Poems,
trans. Pansy Pakenham

Cowley Publications is a ministry of the Society of St. John the Evangelist, a religious community for men in the Episcopal Church. Emerging from the Society's tradition of prayer, theological reflection, and diversity of mission, the press is centered in the rich heritage of the Anglican Communion.

Cowley Publications seeks to provide books, audio cassettes, and other resources for the ongoing theological exploration and spiritual development of the Episcopal Church and others in the body of Christ. To this end, it is dedicated to developing a new generation of theological writers, encouraging them to produce timely, creative, and stimulating publications of excellence, and making these publications available widely, reaching both clergy and lay persons.